The Bea

Author: Karen Kartigan Whiting
Cover and Interior Artist: Corbin Hillam

Copyright © 1997 School Specialty Publishing. Published by Shining Star Publications, an imprint of In Celebration™, a member of the School Specialty Family.

Scripture taken from the HOLY BIBLE: NEW INTERNATIONAL VERSION®. NIV®. Copyright © 1973, 1978, 1984 by International Bible Society. Used by permission of Zondervan Publishing House.

The "NIV" and "New International Version" trademarks are registered in the United States Patent and Trademark Office by International Bible Society.

Send all inquiries to:
In Celebration
3195 Wilson Drive NW
Grand Rapids, Michigan 49544

The Beatitudes

ISBN: 1-56417-955-9

3 4 5 6 7 8 9 10 MAZ 10 09 08 07 06 05

Table of Contents

Shining Star Publications, Copyright © 1998   SS4829

BEATITUDES

To Teachers and Parents

A beatitude is a proclamation of blessings. These words of Jesus help us look beyond pain and problems to promises of future blessings. In a world full of sickness, wars, and natural disasters, children see people break rules, twist truth, and act selfishly. The attitudes Jesus praised bear the fruit of blessings from God.

The activities in this book help children learn by involving them in Bible discovery. The activities cover four topics:

1. The words of each Beatitude (to help students learn and memorize the Scriptures)

2. What each Beatitude means (to identify the attitudes God wants us to develop)

3. Blessings (to identify the future blessings, or fruit described)

4. Related Scriptures (Bible stories, other Scriptures, and looking at the lives of Bible heroes who exemplified the Beatitudes)

Decorate the room with the bulletin board on page 9. Use it to introduce the idea that God blesses us for our attitudes and actions.

Directions for a mobile to reinforce the story start on page 4. When it's completed, children can present the mobile story as a skit to teach others about the Beatitudes.

As you teach the Beatitudes, think of blessings you have received as a result of the right attitude and actions. Ask the Lord to show you any attitudes you need to change. Share with your children how the Beatitudes affect your life. Real life examples show children how we can live what the Bible teaches.

As they do these activities, children should come away with hope and understanding that Jesus wants them to rejoice and be glad. They should also learn that God loves them and wants to bless them.

3

Beatitudes Mobile

Cut a mountain from green poster board. Punch nine holes along the bottom of the mountain and one hole at the top. Attach yarn to the top hole for hanging the mobile.

Cut out and color the Beatitude symbols. Punch a hole in the top of each symbol. Attach the symbols to the mountain with Christmas ornament hangers, yarn, or bent paper clips.

4

SS4829

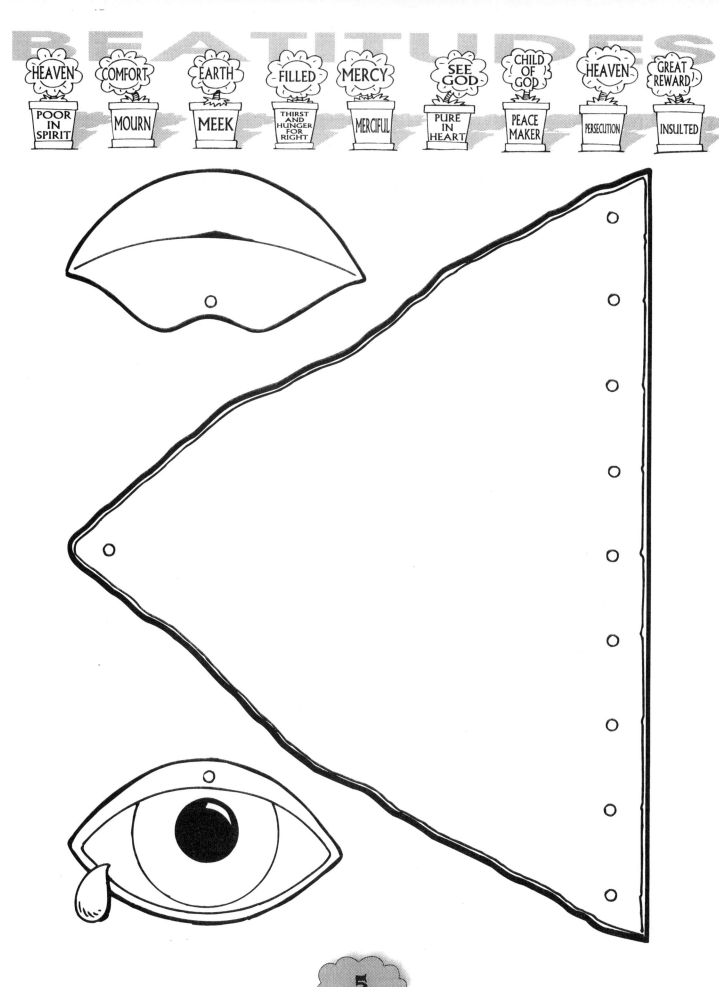

Beatitudes Story/Mobile

Use the Beatitude mobile as a story aid in teaching about the Beatitudes; then let your students make their own mobiles. Read the poem holding up each symbol and attaching it to the mobile after you read the corresponding verse.

High upon a mountain by the sea,
Jesus sat, one bright and sunny day.
His twelve disciples sat down too,
All eager to hear what He would say.

Jesus saw a large crowd gather near.
He chose to teach them a lesson
To ease their troubles and their woes,
His heart filled with love and compassion.

Seeing poor people in the crowd, He said,
"Blessed are the poor in spirit,
For theirs is the kingdom of heaven."
At this, the lights in many hearts were lit.

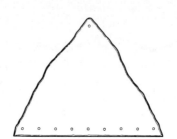

Seeing a young widow's tears, Jesus spoke:
"Blessed are those who mourn,
For they will be comforted;"
And in her heart, new hope was born.

A man who helped the weak heard,
"Blessed are the meek, for they
Will inherit the earth."
He felt the joy of the Lord that day.

The people were hungry and the Lord's words—
"Blessed are those who hunger and thirst
For righteousness, for they will be filled"—
Satisfied those hearts who felt the worst.

"Blessed are the merciful,"
Two heard who were bitter and upset,
"For they will be shown mercy."
And they learned to forgive and forget.

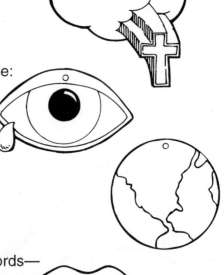

6

SS4829

BEATITUDES

HEAVEN — POOR IN SPIRIT
COMFORT — MOURN
EARTH — MEEK
FILLED — THIRST AND HUNGER FOR RIGHT
MERCY — MERCIFUL
SEE GOD — PURE IN HEART
CHILD OF GOD — PEACE MAKER
HEAVEN — PERSECUTION
GREAT REWARD — INSULTED

"Blessed are the pure in heart,
For they will see God," Jesus said with love.
The people smiled because they knew
His message came from above.

"Blessed are the peacemakers," Jesus said,
While watching some children fight,
"For they will be called sons of God."
The children stopped, to His delight.

"Blessed are those who are persecuted
Because of righteousness," Jesus said,
Then He paused as He saw an honest man
Turn to Him and lift up his head.

"For theirs is the Kingdom of heaven,"
Jesus finished, and the man felt blessed.
In spite of the ridicule and scorn,
He felt ready to again give his best.

"Blessed are you when people persecute you
And accuse you falsely because of Me."
The disciples paid attention to Jesus,
Eager to hear what His next words would be.

"Rejoice and be glad," Jesus declared
To many who listen longer,
"Because great is your reward," He said,
And the words helped hearts grow stronger.

Then Jesus added, "For in the same way
They persecuted the prophets before you."
The disciples though of Elijah and Daniel,
And wanted to remain faithful too.

The crowd was amazed at His Words.
His teachings so honest and pure,
Reached people then and still today
They're changing lives for sure!

7

Beatitudes Logic Problem

Five Christians live in a row. Their names are Juan, Luke, Mary, Martha, and Sally. Each one is an example of someone Jesus spoke about in the Beatitudes. Use the following statements to find out more about each person: the colors of their houses, their Beatitudes and fruit, and where they live on the street.

1. Luke does not live next to Juan or Martha.
2. Juan is a peacemaker and lives next to Mary.
3. Martha does not live next to the person who is mourning.
4. Mary lives in a brown house.
5. The person in the green house will receive mercy and lives next to the orange house.
6. The blue house is next to the red house.
7. The meek person has only one neighbor, who is not the peacemaker.
8. The person in the red house is pure of heart.
9. Sally lives two houses from the person who is mourning.
10. Luke is not mourning.
11. The end houses are blue and green.

SS4829

"Cultivate Blessings" Bulletin Board

Directions:

1. Cover the board with light blue paper.
2. Cut flowerpots from red paper.
3. Write the Beatitude attitude on the pots.
4. Cut flowers and petals from various colors of paper.
5. Write the blessings on the flower centers.

6. Cut stems and leaves from green paper.
7. Cut the letters for the captions from green paper or from pages from a seed or nursery catalog.
8. Mount the caption on the board. Mount each flower and pot as you teach that Beatitude, or put them up all at once.

Shining Star Publications, Copyright © 1998

SS4829

"Jesus—Our Example" Match-ups

Jesus is our example. Look up the Bible verses. Match the characteristic in each Beatitude with an example seen in the life of Christ.

1. Pure in heart	a. John 11:35
2. Meek, attitude of a servant	b. 1 John 3:16
3. Poor in spirit, humble	c. Luke 22:63-65
4. Persecuted because of righteousness	d. John 13:5
5. Insulted for faith	e. Matthew 14:14
6. Peacemaker	f. John 5:30
7. Mourn	g. Phillipians 2:5-8
8. Seek righteousness	h. Matthew 26:51-52
9. Merciful	i. Luke 9:22

10

Poor in Vowels

This Bible verse is poor in vowels. Replace each coin with a vowel to discover one of the Beatitudes.

BL (5¢) SS (5¢) D (25¢) R (5¢) TH (5¢)

P (1¢) (1¢) R (10¢) N SP (10¢) R (10¢) T

F (1¢) R TH (5¢) (10¢) RS (10¢) S

TH (5¢) K (10¢) NGD (1¢) M (1¢) F

H (5¢) (25¢) V (5¢) N.

M (25¢) TTH (5¢) W 5:3

II

SS4829

Centurion Word Search
Based on Matthew 8:5-13

Someone who is poor in spirit is humble. Such a person does not try to have power over other people. He may be important, but he's not bossy. Read this story about a man in the Bible who was poor in spirit. Use the words in the list to complete the sentences. Then find and circle those words in the word search. Some words are used more than once but appear only once in the puzzle.

An _____ man lived in Capernaum. He led 100 soldiers who obeyed him. He was called a _____. He _____ about the people who worked for him. One of his _____ became very sick; he could not walk and felt great pain. The man asked _____ to help. The man was very _____ and said, "_____, I do not _____ to have you come _____ my roof." He _____ Jesus only _____ to say the word and his servant would be _____. He explained that he understood _____. He _____ and gave orders. When he gave _____, he expected his workers to _____. Jesus was _____. "I have not _____ anyone in Israel with such great _____," Jesus said. He told the centurion to _____. At that very _____ the man's servant was _____.

```
B L E S S A U T H O R I T Y E
J D C F O L L O W E D A R E D
E T A S T O N I S H E D H R E
S E R V A N T S T E R U O H L
U P E O O R I I E N S L R H A
S P D O I R A I T V T H D U E
E I B R S F O U N D R I E M H
C E N T U R I O N S K E R B I
Y N B E L I E V E D G D S L G
O I M P O R T A N T E M O E O
F H N E E D E D E A V R E N D
```

Word List

ASTONISHED	FOLLOWED	JESUS
AUTHORITY	FOUND	LORD
BELIEVED	GO	NEEDED
CARED	HEALED	OBEY
CENTURION	HOUR	ORDERS
DESERVE	HUMBLE	SERVANTS
FAITH	IMPORTANT	UNDER

Write the uncircled letters in the word search on the lines below to discover one of the Beatitudes.

__ __ __ __ __ __ __ __ __ __ __ __ __ __ __ __ __ __ __ __

__ __ __ __ __ __ __ FOR __ __ __ __ __ __ __ __ __ __

THE __ __ __ __ __ __ __ __ __ __ __ __ __ __ __ __.

12

SS4829

The Spirit of the Game

Before playing, fill in the game squares with arrows to show which direction to move. Use arrows pointing forward for Bible heroes who were poor in spirit. Use backward arrows for Bible people who were proud. Look up the Bible verses if you're not sure.

To play, use buttons for markers. Roll a die for how many squares to move. Follow instructions on the squares. See who can reach the kingdom of heaven first!

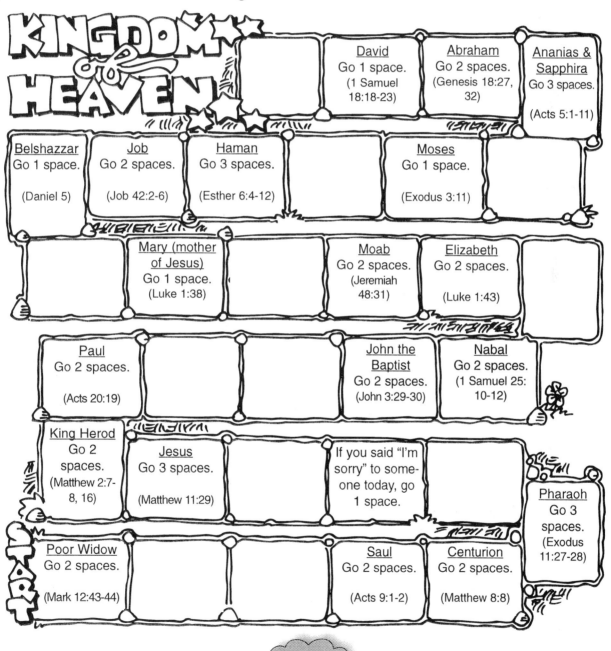

KINGDOM OF HEAVEN

David
Go 1 space.
(1 Samuel 18:18-23)

Abraham
Go 2 spaces.
(Genesis 18:27, 32)

Ananias & Sapphira
Go 3 spaces.
(Acts 5:1-11)

Belshazzar
Go 1 space.
(Daniel 5)

Job
Go 2 spaces.
(Job 42:2-6)

Haman
Go 3 spaces.
(Esther 6:4-12)

Moses
Go 1 space.
(Exodus 3:11)

Mary (mother of Jesus)
Go 1 space.
(Luke 1:38)

Moab
Go 2 spaces.
(Jeremiah 48:31)

Elizabeth
Go 2 spaces.
(Luke 1:43)

Paul
Go 2 spaces.
(Acts 20:19)

John the Baptist
Go 2 spaces.
(John 3:29-30)

Nabal
Go 2 spaces.
(1 Samuel 25: 10-12)

King Herod
Go 2 spaces.
(Matthew 2:7-8, 16)

Jesus
Go 3 spaces.
(Matthew 11:29)

If you said "I'm sorry" to someone today, go 1 space.

Pharaoh
Go 3 spaces.
(Exodus 11:27-28)

START

Poor Widow
Go 2 spaces.
(Mark 12:43-44)

Saul
Go 2 spaces.
(Acts 9:1-2)

Centurion
Go 2 spaces.
(Matthew 8:8)

13

SS4829

Notes of Comfort

The Bible is filled with messages of comfort from God. When you feel sad, read the Bible! God's words will lift you up, comfort you, and encourage you like nothing else can.

Laminate this page by covering it with adhesive plastic. Cut out the messages of comfort below. Punch a hole in the end of each one and put them all on a metal ring. Keep them handy so you can refer to one when you feel down.

"I have told you these things, so that in me you may have peace. In this world you will have trouble. But take heart! I have overcome the world." John 16:33
"Praise be to the God and Father of our Lord Jesus Christ, the Father of compassion and the God of all comfort." 2 Corinthians 1:3
"Blessed are those who mourn, for they will be comforted." Matthew 5:4
"But now, Lord, what do I look for? My hope is in you." Psalm 39:7
"Ask and it will be given to you; seek and you will find; knock and the door will be opened to you." Matthew 7:7
"He gives strength to the weary and increases the power of the weak." Isaiah 40:29
"But those who hope in the Lord will renew their strength. They will soar on wings like eagles; they will run and not grow weary, they will walk and not be faint." Isaiah 40:31
"Let us not become weary in doing good, for at the proper time we will reap a harvest if we do not give up." Galatians 6:9
"Dear friends, let us love one another, for love comes from God. Everyone who loves has been born of God and knows God." 1 John 4:7
"How great is the love the Father has lavished on us, that we should be called children of God! And that is what we are! The reason the world does not know us is that it did not know him." 1 John 3:1
"For God so loved the world that he gave his one and only Son, that whoever believes in him shall not perish but have eternal life." John 3:16
"The thief comes only to steal and kill and destroy; I have come that they may have life, and have it to the full." John 10:10

SS4829

HEAVEN — POOR IN SPIRIT | COMFORT — MOURN | EARTH — MEEK | FILLED — THIRST AND HUNGER FOR RIGHT | MERCY — MERCIFUL | SEE GOD — PURE IN HEART | CHILD OF GOD — PEACE MAKER | HEAVEN — PERSECUTION | GREAT REWARD — INSULTED

Pyramid Puzzle

Fit the sixteen triangles into the pyramid. Then read across, from top to bottom, to find a Beatitude. Do not rotate any of the triangles. (You may want to cut out the triangles and move them around to help solve the puzzle.)

SS4829

Comforting Word Search
Based on John 11:1–45

Mary and Martha asked Jesus to help when their brother, Lazarus, was sick, but Lazarus died. Mary and Martha mourned. These two sisters were friends of Jesus. Complete the sentences about what Jesus did to comfort them. Look up the Bible verses in the Gospel of John to check your answers. Circle the words in the puzzle as you find them.

1. Lazarus was __ __ __ __. (11:1)
2. Mary __ __ __ __ __ __ perfume on the Lord. (11:2)
3. Mary __ __ __ __ __ the Lord's feet with her hair. (11:2)
4. Mary and Martha sent this message to Jesus: "Lord, the one you __ __ __ __ is sick." (11:3)
5. Jesus loved __ __ __ __ __ __. (11:5)
6. __ __ __ __ __ stayed where He was for two more days. (11:6)
7. The disciples called Jesus, __ __ __ __ __. (11:8)
8. Jesus said, "Our __ __ __ __ __ __, Lazarus, has fallen asleep, but I am going there to __ __ __ __ him up." (11:11)
9. Jesus did not __ __ __ __ __ __ until Lazarus had been __ __ __ __ four days. (11:17)
10. Many Jews had come to __ __ __ __ __ __ __ __ Mary and Martha. (11:19)
11. Jesus told Martha that her brother would __ __ __ __ again. (11:23)
12. Jesus said, "I am the resurrection and the __ __ __ __." (11:25)
13. "Yes, Lord," Martha told Jesus, "I __ __ __ __ __ __ __ __ that you are the __ __ __ __ __ __." (11:27)
14. When Jesus went to Lazarus' tomb, He was deeply __ __ __ __ __. (11:33)
15. Jesus __ __ __ __. (11:35)
16. People asked if Jesus could not have __ __ __ __ Lazarus from dying. (11:37)
17. Jesus said, "If you believed, you would __ __ __ the __ __ __ __ __ of God." (11:40)
18. Jesus prayed, "Father I __ __ __ __ __ you that you have heard me." (11:41)
19. Jesus said His words to the Father were to help, or __ __ __ __ __ __ __ __ the people. (11:42)
20. Jesus called, "Lazarus, __ __ __ __ out." (11:43)
21. When Lazarus came out, his __ __ __ __ __ and feet were wrapped with strips of linen. (11:44)
22. Many Jews who saw Jesus raise Lazarus put their __ __ __ __ __ in Him. (11:45)

The letters not circled in the puzzle spell out a secret message. The message tells what Jesus said would happen to people who mourn.

___ ___ ___ ___ ___ ___ ___ ___ ___

___ ___ ___ ___ ___ ___

F	T	P	E	W	R	I	S	E	E	O	R
T	H	P	B	E	L	I	E	V	E	E	Y
L	I	F	E	W	C	I	I	O	L	L	D
T	H	A	N	K	Y	R	O	L	G	N	E
M	B	C	E	E	R	S	U	S	E	J	R
O	A	H	F	A	I	T	H	I	M	E	U
V	C	R	I	B	B	A	R	O	O	K	O
E	M	I	T	R	O	F	M	O	C	A	P
D	F	S	O	H	R	D	E	P	I	W	T
E	D	T	D	E	A	D	H	A	N	D	S

16

"Mourning" Acrostic

Throughout the Bible, people mourned. Discover some of those people from the clues below. The letters in the boxes will spell out what those who mourn will receive.

___ ___ [ ] ___ ___ mourned the loss of his son. (Genesis 37:34-35)

___ [ ] ___ lost all his children, money, and health. (James 5:11)

___ ___ ___ [ ] and ___ ___ ___ lost their first son. (Genesis 4:25)

The lost son's [ ] ___ ___ ___ ___ ___ (Luke 15:20)

___ ___ [ ] ___ Her husband and two sons died. (Ruth 1:5)

___ ___ [ ] ___ mourned the death of Jesus. (John 20:10-16)

___ ___ [ ] ___ ___ Her brother died. (John 11:21-22)

SS4829

"Blessed Are the Meek" Booklet

Meek people treat other people and the earth with gentle care. Make this booklet as a reminder of what the meek will inherit. The verses on the pages are from the Psalms to help us praise God for the earth He made. (If you copy the pages, make sure you copy pages 19-20 on the front and back of one sheet correctly lined up.)

Directions:

1. Color the pages as follows:
   page 3 green
   page 5 light blue
   page 7 brown
   page 9 green with red apples
   page 11 purple
   page 15 blue
2. Cut out the double pages along the solid lines.
   Cut out the oval on page 2.

3. Fold on the dotted lines.
4. Assemble the pages in order and staple them together.
5. Write or paste the verse on the cover.
   Cover verse:

   "Blessed are the meek for they will inherit the earth." Matthew 5:5

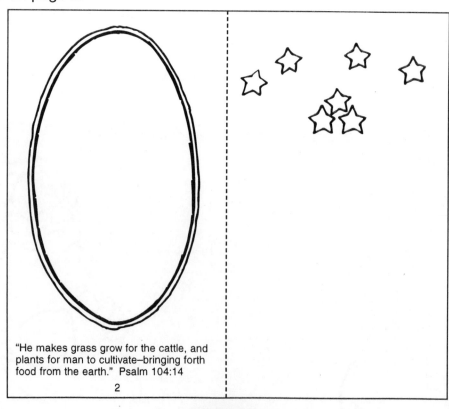

"He makes grass grow for the cattle, and plants for man to cultivate–bringing forth food from the earth." Psalm 104:14

2

18

SS4829

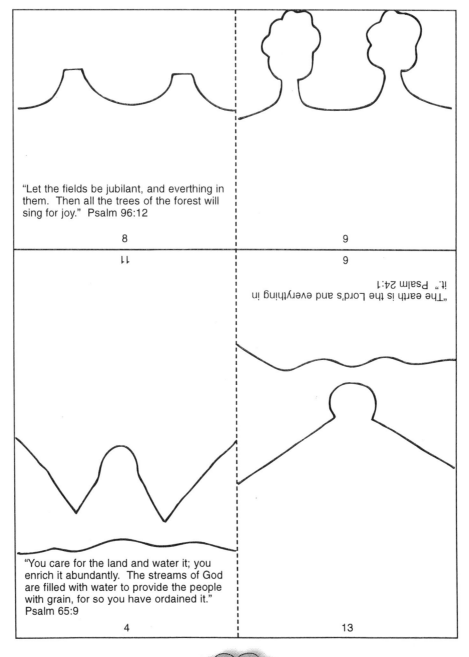

"Let the fields be jubilant, and everthing in them. Then all the trees of the forest will sing for joy." Psalm 96:12

8

9

11

6

"The earth is the Lord's and everything in it." Psalm 24:1

"You care for the land and water it; you enrich it abundantly. The streams of God are filled with water to provide the people with grain, for so you have ordained it." Psalm 65:9

4

13

19

"Your righteousness is like the mighty
mountains, your justice like the great
deep." Psalm 36:6

10

7

5

12

"[Who made] the moon and the stars to
govern the night; his love endures
forever." Psalm 136:9

"Your love, O Lord, reaches to the
heavens, your faithfulness to the skies."
Psalm 36:5

14

3

20

SS4829

BEATITUDES

HEAVEN — POOR IN SPIRIT
COMFORT — MOURN
EARTH — MEEK
FILLED — THIRST AND HUNGER FOR RIGHT
MERCY — MERCIFUL
SEE GOD — PURE IN HEART
CHILD OF GOD — PEACE MAKER
HEAVEN — PERSECUTION
GREAT REWARD — INSULTED

How to Be Meek

Jesus said, "Blessed are the meek," but what does it mean to be meek? How can a person learn to be meek? Jesus was meek, willing to give up power and die for us.

Look up the Bible verses to find words that fit the acrostic. Each word shows another quality of a meek person. Then read the words inside the cross.

___ ___ ___ ___ ___ ___   Matthew 11:29

___ ___ ___ ___ ___ ___ ___ ___   2 Corinthians 9:11

M E E K

___ ___ ___ ___ ___ ___ ___ ___ ___   Collosians 3:12

___ ___ ___ ___ ___   1 Peter 3:4

___ ___ ___ ___ ___ ___ ___   1 Timothy 2:11

___ ___ ___ ___ ___ ___   1 Corinthians 13:4

Proverbs 2:2   ___ ___ ___ ___ ___ ___ ___ ___ ___

___ ___ ___   Ephesians 4:32

___ ___ ___ ___   Mark 12:30

21

SS4829

Fractioned Verse

A Beatitude is hidden in the other words below. Solve the fractions to find the ten words to make the verse. Then read from top to bottom to find out what blessing people who do not seek power will receive. Read Matthew 5:5 to check your work.

1. First ½ of be + first ⅔ of lesson + last ⅓ of prayed = _____

2. The middle ½ of Mark + first ⅙ of Exodus = _____

3. The last ⅓ of hat + the first ½ of head = _____

4. Third and fourth ⅕ of James + third and fourth ⅐ of Ezekiel = _____

5. First 3/7 of forgive = _____

6. First 3/13 of Thessalonians + last ⅓ of joy = _____

7. First ¾ of wilt + first ¼ of love = _____

8. Second and third ⅕ of Kings + last ½ of Esther + second and third ⅕ of Titus = _____

9. Last ½ of Ruth + first ⅑ of Ephesians = _____

10. The last ⅘ of heart + first ½ of hi = _____

SS4829

Righteousness Crossword Puzzle

Look up the Bible verses on righteousness to complete the sentence and fill in the crossword puzzle.

Across

3. "You have loved righteousness and hated wickedness; therefore God, your God, has set you above your companions by anointing you with the _____." (Hebrews 1:9)

4. "But you, man of god, flee from all this, and _____ righteousness, godliness, faith, love, endurance, and gentleness." (1 Timothy 6:11)

6. "But seek _____ his kingdom and his righteousness, and all these things will be given to you as well." (Matthew 6:33)

7. "Righteousness will be his belt and _____ the sash around his waist." (Isaiah 11:5)

11. "The wicked man flees though no one pursues, but the righteous are as _____as a lion." (Proverbs 28:1)

12. "They will go away to eternal punishment, but the righteous to eternal _____." (Matthew 25:46)

13. "Consider Abraham: 'He _____ God, and it was credited to him as righteousness.'" (Galatians 3:6)

Down

1. "Those who are wise will shine like the brightness of the heavens, and those who lead many to righteousness, like the _____ for ever and ever." (Daniel 12:3)

2. "Glorious and majestic are his deeds, and his righteousness endures _____." (Psalm 111:3)

4. "Therefore confess your sins to each other and pray for each other that you may be healed. The prayer of a righteous man is _____ and effective." (James 5:16)

5. "The Lord is far from the wicked but he hears the _____ of the righteous." (Proverbs 15:29)

8. "Whoever trusts in his riches will fall, but the righteous will _____ like a green leaf." (Proverbs 11:28)

9. "If we confess our sins, he is faithful and just and will _____ us our sins and purify us from all unrighteousness." (1 John 1:9)

10. "This is the account of Noah. Noah was a righteous man, blameless among the people of his time, and he _____ with God." (Genesis 6:9)

23

Balanced Meals Place Mat

Make a place mat to help you remember that you need a balanced spiritual diet.

Materials:

    paper
    pen
    crayons or markers

Directions:

1. Write out Matthew 5:6 across the top of the paper.
2. Draw a plate on the place mat and list on it ways to be spiritually filled. (Examples: prayer, Bible study)
3. Draw a cup and write on it where you can find truth or righteousness. (Example: the Bible)
4. Draw eating utensils (spoon, fork, knife) and write on them names of people who can help you find truth. (Example: your pastor)
5. Draw or glue pictures of food along the sides of the place mat.
6. When your place mat is done, put it inside a plastic food storage bag and tape it closed. Use it with your meals at home.

24

Seeking Righteousness

Follow the directions to decode the Bible verse.

1	2	3	4	5	6	7	8	9	10	11	12	13
T	R	U	H	A	B	C	D	E	F	G	I	J

14	15	16	17	18	19	20	21	22	23	24	25	26
K	L	M	N	O	P	Q	S	V	W	X	Y	Z

1. Add 1 to each number; then match it to the letter in the code.

   $\overline{}$ $\overline{}$ $\overline{}$ $\overline{}$ $\overline{}$ $\overline{}$ $\overline{}$ $\overline{}$ $\overline{}$ $\overline{}$ $\overline{}$ $\overline{}$ $\overline{}$ $\overline{}$ $\overline{}$
    5 14 8 20 20 8 7   4 1 8   0 3 17 20 8

2. Divide each number by 2; then match it to the letter in the code.

   $\overline{}$ $\overline{}$ $\overline{}$ $\overline{}$ $\overline{}$ $\overline{}$ $\overline{}$ $\overline{}$ $\overline{}$
    46 8 36   8 6 34 22 18 4

3. Use every third number; then match it to the letter in the code.

   $\overline{}$ $\overline{}$ $\overline{}$ $\overline{}$ $\overline{}$ $\overline{}$ $\overline{}$ $\overline{}$ $\overline{}$
   1-2-5 3-4-17 5-6-8   20-2-1 7-8-4 10-11-12 4-4-2 28-99-21 1-2-1

4. Subtract 1 from each number; then match it to the letter in the code.

   $\overline{}$ $\overline{}$ $\overline{}$ $\overline{}$ $\overline{}$ $\overline{}$ $\overline{}$ $\overline{}$ $\overline{}$ $\overline{}$ $\overline{}$ $\overline{}$ $\overline{}$ $\overline{}$
    11 19 3   3 13 12 5 2 10 19 4 22 18 10 22 22

5. Subtract 4 from each number; then match it to the letter in the code.

   $\overline{}$ $\overline{}$ $\overline{}$ $\overline{}$ $\overline{}$ $\overline{}$ $\overline{}$
    14 22 6   5 8 13 29

6. Add each number to the number represented by the letter; then match it to the letter in the code.

     22 10 12 14   2 8   8 9 14 11 8 6
   + T R U T   H T   R U T H T R
   _____

   = $\overline{}$ $\overline{}$ $\overline{}$ $\overline{}$ $\overline{}$ $\overline{}$ $\overline{}$ $\overline{}$ $\overline{}$ $\overline{}$ $\overline{}$

25

SS4829

Food for Thought

Unscramble the words to find some things Jesus was compared to. Look up the Bible verses to discover how He was compared to them.

r b d a e = _ _ _ _ _ John 6:51

t r e w a = _ _ _ _ _ John 4:10

n e v i = _ _ _ _ John 15:1

m l a b = _ _ _ _ John 1:29

t h e w a = _ _ _ _ _ John 12:23-24

What do these five things have in common? What do you hunger and thirst for? Read Matthew 5:6. If you hunger and thirst for righteousness, what do you think God will fill you with?

26

Full Circle Coded Fun

When we are merciful, it circles back to us, and we receive mercy. Fill out the words in the wheel, going into the center. Then read around the wheel to find a Bible verse about mercy.

1. Opposite of after
2. Opposite of late
3. What Mary did at the feet of Jesus (Luke 10:39)
4. Joseph interpreted one for Pharaoh (Genesis 41:17-32)
5. Small city, Bethlehem was one (John 7:42)
6. Black water snake
7. Rahab used a scarlet cord, or _____ to signal Joshua's men. (Joshua 2)
8. God's purpose, or _____ (Ephesians 3:10)

27

SS4829

HEAVEN — POOR IN SPIRIT
COMFORT — MOURN
EARTH — MEEK
FILLED — THIRST AND HUNGER FOR RIGHT
MERCY — MERCIFUL
SEE GOD — PURE IN HEART
CHILD OF GOD — PEACE MAKER
HEAVEN — PERSECUTION
GREAT REWARD — INSULTED

Making Choices About Helping

Read the Good Samaritan parable in Luke 10:30-37. Then choose the right ending to each sentence.

1. A man was traveling
   a. to the movies.
   b. to the Sea of Galilee.
   c. from Jerusalem to Jericho.

2. The man
   a. visited a friend.
   b. ate an ice-cream cone.
   c. was robbed.

3. A priest saw the man and
   a. passed him by.
   b. robbed him.
   c. took care of him.

4. A Levite saw the man and
   a. laughed at him.
   b. called 911.
   c. passed him by.

5. A Samaritan saw the man and
   a. passed by on the other side of the road.
   b. took pity on him.
   c. chased the robbers away.

6. The Samaritan went to the man and
   a. gave him money.
   b. tickled him.
   c. bandaged his wounds.

7. The Samaritan poured something on the wounds. It was
   a. iodine.
   b. oil and water.
   c. oil and wine.

8. He took the man to
   a. a hospital.
   b. an inn.
   c. to see Jesus.

9. The man's neighbor was
   a. the robbers.
   b. the one who showed him mercy.
   c. the lawyer.

10. Jesus told the lawyer to
   a. go and do likewise.
   b. tell the parable to other people.
   c. take a trip to Disney World.

The people in the parable made choices about showing mercy. We must make choices when someone needs help too. Pray and ask Jesus to help you make the right choice when you see someone who needs help.

28

SS4829

"Be Merciful" Bingo

Here are some ways to show mercy. Take the bingo card home and do some of the things. Bring the card back with five in a row marked off.

M	E	R	C	Y
Forgive someone who hurt you.	Help a friend.	Give food to someone who is needy.	Pray for someone who is sick.	Send a letter to a sick friend.
Make a snack for Mom or Dad.	Write to a missionary.	Tell someone about Jesus.	Say thank you to everyone who helps you.	Send a card to an older person from your church.
Help your teacher clean the classroom.	Invite someone to Sunday School.	Free Space ★ GOD'S ★ Mercy is free!	Help with the dishes.	Put out crumbs or seeds for the birds.
Read a story to a little child.	Give everyone you see a beautiful smile.	Memorize Matthew 5:7.	Visit a widow or someone who is lonely.	Help cook supper.
Give Dad or Mom a back rub.	Pray for poor people around the world.	Help watch a neighbor's child.	Cheer up a sad friend.	Give your teacher a hug.

29

SS4829

Hands of Mercy

There are many ways to show mercy to people. To show mercy is to be kind and forgiving.

"Be kind and compassionate to one another, forgiving each other, just as in Christ God forgave you." Ephesians 4:32

Make these helpful hands of mercy as a reminder to reach out to others with mercy.

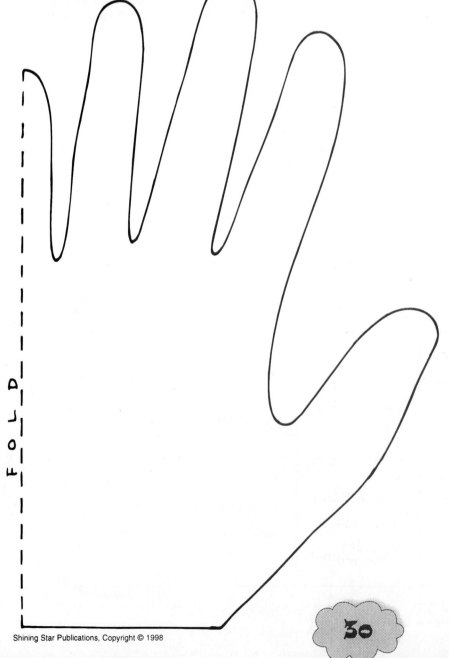

FOLD

Directions:

1. Place your hand on a folded paper, with your little finger on the fold. Trace your hand and cut it out, being careful not to cut along the folded edge.

2. On the closed hand, write names of people for whom you will pray. (These may be people you need to forgive, people you need to try to be kinder to, or people who need help.)

3. Open up the hand. Inside, write things you will do for other people to show mercy. (Examples: hugging, shaking hands, doing things for people)

30

SS4829

Pocketful of Heart

Color and cut out the hearts. Glue the edges below the dots together, forming a pocket. Color and cut out the picture. Place the picture inside the pocket. Carry it with you to remind you of the Bible verse, "Blessed are the pure in heart, for they will see God."

HEAVEN • POOR IN SPIRIT
COMFORT • MOURN
EARTH • MEEK
FILLED • THIRST AND HUNGER FOR RIGHT
MERCY • MERCIFUL
SEE GOD • PURE IN HEART
CHILD OF GOD • PEACE MAKER
HEAVEN • PERSECUTION
GREAT REWARD • INSULTED

"Seeing God" Activities
Pass the Secret Message!

Materials:

waxed paper
paper
pencil
crayon

Directions:

1. Place waxed paper on top of the plain paper.

2. Using a pencil, write out Matthew 5:8 on the waxed paper. (Bear down hard on the pencil.)

3. Give the plain paper to a friend who doesn't know Jesus. Explain that there's a secret message on the paper. All he has to do is rub a crayon over the paper and the message will appear!

A "Seeing" Heart

Jesus tells us that those who are pure in heart will see God. Not only will they see Him in heaven someday, but they will also "see" Him or learn to know Him better now. Put a paper heart in plain sight in the room (not in an obvious place) before students enter. Tell them that they should go in and remain standing until they see the heart. As soon as they see it, they should sit down (but not point it out to anyone else). Talk about how we often don't notice things that are right in front of us in plain view. Jesus promised that people who are pure in heart will be aware of God and "see" Him with their hearts.

Blessed are the pure in heart for they will see GOD

32

SS4829

Searching Hearts

God searches our hearts. Use the letter graph to discover a message from the Bible about hearts. For each letter, find the first letter in the left column of the graph. Then go right to the column under the letter from hearts. For example, GE represents the letter B. Check your answer by reading Matthew 5:8.

	H	E	A	R	T	S
G	A	B	D	E	G	H
O	I	L	N	O	P	R
D	S	T	U	W	F	Y

GE OE GR DH DH GR GA   GH OS GR   DE GS GR

___ __ __ __ __ __ __   __ __ __   __ __ __

OT DA OS GR   OH OA   GS GR GH OS DE   DT OR OS

__ __ __ __   __ __   __ __ __ __ __,   __ __ __

DE GS GR DS   DR OH OE OE   DH GR GR   GT OR GA

__ __ __ __   __ __ __ __   __ __ __   __ __ __.

33

HEAVEN · COMFORT · EARTH · FILLED · MERCY · SEE GOD · CHILD OF GOD · HEAVEN · GREAT REWARD

POOR IN SPIRIT · MOURN · MEEK · THIRST AND HUNGER FOR RIGHT · MERCIFUL · PURE IN HEART · PEACE MAKER · PERSECUTION · INSULTED

Recipe for a Pure Heart

Do you want to see God someday? Jesus said people who are pure in heart will. How does one get a pure heart? Decode the ingredients and follow the recipe. Use the code wheel to discover the ingredients. Dial until you come to a stop. Each ingredient is paired with a Bible verse about that ingredient.

Mix together:

___ ___ ___ ___ ___   Start at 1 and pick up every other letter. (Acts 15:9)

___ ___ ___ ___   Start at 2 and pick up every second letter. (1 John 3:3)

___ ___ ___ ___ ___ ___ ___ God's ___ ___ ___ ___.   Start at 3 and pick up every other letter. (1 Peter 1:22)

Add:

Daily prayer and Bible reading.
Heat with the warmth of God's love.
Once the heart is made pure, fill it with LOVE.
This serves enough to last one person for a lifetime.

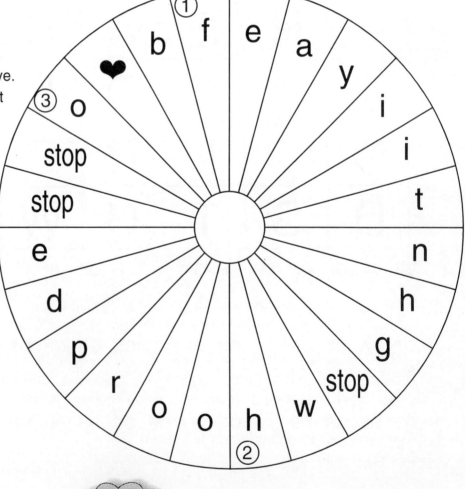

34

SS4829

"Cut and Tell" Peace Skit

Directions:

Fold a circle of paper three times (forming eighths). Draw lines, following the pattern. Each person cuts one piece, then talks while unfolding it. Let one person be Christian and pantomime the actions. The skit uses seven people.

One (Cuts and holds up the one): One day, one person opened his heart and saw the message of the cross (opens the one to reveal cross). He believed in Jesus. (Christian folds his hands in prayer, then puts the cross in a pocket or pins it on his shirt.) This person became known as a Christian.

Dove (cuts and holds up dove): Christian prayed and heard God speak. God spoke to his heart and through the Bible. God pointed to the birds, especially the dove, and told how they spread beauty to the four corners of the world. (Cut apart four doves; fold open the wings, and let Christian give them to people in four corners of the room.) The dove, a symbol of God's Spirit, is also a symbol for love and peace. God wanted Christian, like the birds, to spread His love everywhere to give peace to others.

Hearts (Two people each cut and hold up a set of folded hearts, holding them like shoes)

Heart 1 So Christian obeyed, and picked up his feet to go and spread God's love (opens up one set of hearts). Christian passed God's love to everyone. Some people accepted God's love. Those who accepted God's love, in turn, passed God's love to more people. (Christian passes out the hearts.)

Heart 2 (Opens up other set of hearts): Christian spent a lifetime spreading God's love, praying that all people would accept it. Everywhere, Christian found some people who received God's love, though others did not. (Christian passes out two hearts, and lets two fall to the floor.)

35

BEATITUDES

HEAVEN · COMFORT · EARTH · FILLED · MERCY · SEE GOD · CHILD OF GOD · HEAVEN · GREAT REWARD

POOR IN SPIRIT · MOURN · MEEK · THIRST AND HUNGER FOR RIGHT · MERCIFUL · PURE IN HEART · PEACE MAKER · PERSECUTION · INSULTED

People (Cut out and hold up closed circle of people): How happy Christian felt when even one person accepted God's love! Christian saw that those who accepted God's love were joined together with love (open up circle and point to open hearts connecting the people). These people learned to live together in peace. (Christian points to circle and smiles.)

Crown (Cuts and holds up folded crown): One day God called Christian home to heaven. God said, "Christian, blessed are you, for you have been a peacemaker. You are My child. Every child of the King is a prince or princess. Therefore, wear this crown, Christian." (Open up the crown, and place on the head of the person who passed out the hearts.)

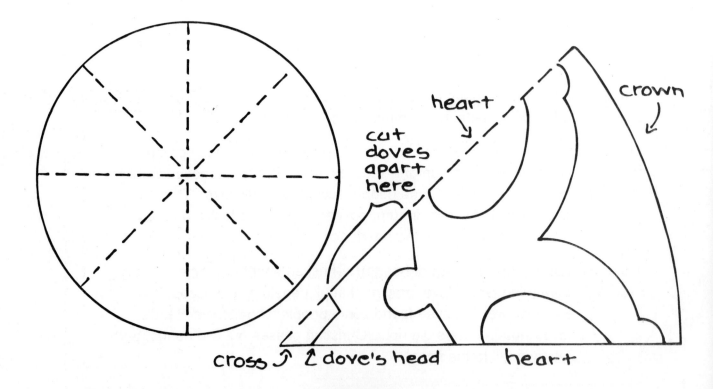

heart

crown

cut doves apart here

cross ↗ ↖ dove's head   heart

Shining Star Publications, Copyright © 1998

SS4829

Peace Tree Bulletin Board

In Sweden, boys and girls make peace trees at Christmas to symbolize peace on earth. Have students decorate a peace tree bulletin board to remind them that peace begins in our hearts.

Directions:

Cover the board with blue paper. Cut out a green flowerpot for the base. Use brown strips of paper to make the latticework for the tree. Cut one long trunk and four crossbars, each one shorter than the one below it. Write the Bible verse across the top of the bulletin board.

1. **Boy and Girl Figures:** Have each student cut out and color a paper girl or boy, using the patterns on page 38. Let each write on the figure the name of a place in the world where children live in the midst of fighting,. Ask the students to pray for children in the country they chose. Hang the figures on the top and third branches of the tree.

2. **Bells:** Make several bells, using the pattern on page 38. Write on them songs and Bible verses about peace. We need to be messengers of peace, like the angels at Jesus' birth. Take time to sing one of the songs or read some of the Bible verses. Hang the bells on the second branch.

3. **Apples:** Cut out and color nine copies of the apple on page 38. Write the Fruit of the Spirit (Galatians 5:22-23) on them. As God's peacemakers, we need these fruit. Hang eight of the apples on the ends of the branches. Hang the last one on the bottom center branch.

4. **Hearts:** Copy and color the hearts, using the pattern on page 38. Write on the hearts ways Jesus gives us peace. Place these on either side of the apples across the bottom branch.

5. **Star:** Cut out and color a large star for the treetop. Write "Jesus, Prince of Peace" on the star. Read Isaiah 9:6.

"Blessed are the peacemakers, for they will be called sons of God." Matthew 5:9

SS4829

Peace Tree Patterns

SS4829

HEAVEN · COMFORT · EARTH · FILLED · MERCY · SEE GOD · CHILD OF GOD · HEAVEN · GREAT REWARD!

POOR IN SPIRIT · MOURN · MEEK · THIRST AND HUNGER FOR RIGHT · MERCIFUL · PURE IN HEART · PEACE MAKER · PERSECUTION · INSULTED

Peacemaker Hall of Fame

Here are some Bible people who belong in the Peacemaker Hall of Fame for their peacemaking efforts. Unscramble the letters to discover their names. Look up the Bible verses to discover what they did as peacemakers.

1. Tried to make peace between his father and his friend (1 Samuel 19:1-7)

   N T A H J N O A = __ __ __ __ __ __ __ __

2. Peacemaker between believers in Jerusalem (Acts 12:17)

   A S M J E = __ __ __ __ __

3. Peacemaker between the rich and poor of his people (Nehemiah 5:1-13)

   E E A H H N M I = __ __ __ __ __ __ __ __

4. Made peace with his brother (Genesis 32:6–33:5)

   C B J O A = __ __ __ __ __

5. Wanted peace with his brother and their families (Genesis 13:8)

   B A R M A = __ __ __ __ __

6. Tried to make peace with the leader of a country (Exodus 5:1-2; 10:24-27)

   S E O M S = __ __ __ __ __

7. Made the first peace treaty (Genesis 21:22-24)

   E C E L A H B I M = __ __ __ __ __ __ __ __ __

8. Tried to make peace between her husband and a king (1 Samuel 25:14-35)

   I I G A L B A = __ __ __ __ __ __ __

9. Made a peaceful agreement to obtain a wife (Ruth 4:10)

   Z B A O = __ __ __ __

10. Made peace for the nation over dinner (Esther 7:1-8)

    H S E R T E = __ __ __ __ __ __

11. Chosen to keep peace among the people (Judges 2:7)

    R D E L E S = __ __ __ __ __ __

Shining Star Publications, Copyright © 1998

SS4829

Singing While Persecuted

Paul was thrown into prison for his faith in Jesus. So what did he do? He sang! Why? He knew a secret. Use the musical notes to complete what Paul knew. Read Matthew 5:10 to check your work.

Shining Star Publications, Copyright © 1998

SS4829

BEATITUDES

HEAVEN — POOR IN SPIRIT
COMFORT — MOURN
EARTH — MEEK
FILLED — THIRST AND HUNGER FOR RIGHT
MERCY — MERCIFUL
SEE GOD — PURE IN HEART
CHILD OF GOD — PEACE MAKER
HEAVEN — PERSECUTION
GREAT REWARD — INSULTED

Persecution Stress Wheel

Look at the wheel for some suggestions to relieve stress. Make it and use it when you feel persecuted for your faith.

Go for a brisk walk or bike ride.

Listen to Christian music.

Sing a song or read a joke.

Read a Psalm.

Relax.

Talk to a Christian friend.

Pray; tell Jesus how you feel.

Ask a friend to pray with you.

Directions:
1. Cut out the wheel.
2. Glue it on cardboard.
3. Cut or punch a hole in the center.
4. Place a pencil point in the hole to make a spinner.
5. Spin the wheel. Do the activity that appears in front of you.
6. If you still feel stressed, give the wheel another spin and try another activity.

41

SS4829

HEAVEN — POOR IN SPIRIT
COMFORT — MOURN
EARTH — MEEK
FILLED — THIRST AND HUNGER FOR RIGHT
MERCY — MERCIFUL
SEE GOD — PURE IN HEART
CHILD OF GOD — PEACE MAKER
HEAVEN — PERSECUTION
GREAT REWARD — INSULTED

"Paul's Problems" Acrostic

Paul suffered for his faith. Fill in the acrostic, following the clues to learn about Paul. Look up the Bible verses if you need help. The letters in the squares spell out a word for Paul's suffering.

1. This happened to Paul when he rode in boats, three times! (2 Corinthians 11:25)
2. Severely whipped (2 Corinthians 11:23)
3. Taken to be put in prison (Acts 21:33)
4. Paul received 39 of these from a whip. (2 Corinthians 11:24)
5. Pulled along the ground (Acts 14:19)
6. Bound or fastened (Acts 16:26)
7. Falsely charged (Acts 22:30)
8. Clothes removed (Acts 16:22)
9. Grabbed (Acts 24:6)
10. Hit with rocks (2 Corinthians 11:25)
11. Body hit repeatedly (2 Corinthians 11:25)

1. ___ ___ ___ ___ ___ ___ ___ ___ ___
2. ___ ___ ___ ___ ___ ___ ___
3. ___ ___ ___ ___ ___ ___
4. ___ ___ ___ ___ ___
5. ___ ___ ___ ___ ___
6. ___ ___ ___ ___ ___ ___
7. ___ ___ ___ ___ ___
8. ___ ___ ___ ___
9. ___ ___ ___ ___
10. ___ ___ ___ ___ ___
11. ___ ___ ___ ___ ___

42

SS4829

Reactions to Persecution

Read each statement; then decide if it is true or false. If it is true, circle the letter under the true column. If false, circle the letter under the false column. Look up the Bible verses if you need help.

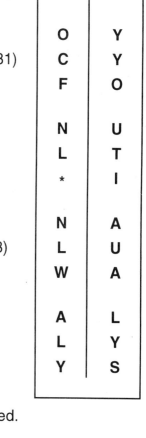

Statement	TRUE	FALSE
1. God allowed Satan to persecute Job. (Job 1:8-12)	B	P
2. When Stephen was stoned, he asked God to save his friend. (Acts 7:59)	R	E
Shadrach, Meshach, and Abednego were thrown into a furnace. They told the king that even if God did not save them, they would not worship the king's statue. (Daniel 3:18)	J	A
4. Paul and Silas prayed and sang in prison. (Acts 16:25)	O	Y
5. Isaac's enemies were jealous and never made peace with him. (Genesis 26:31)	C	Y
6. When the disciple John was exiled, God used him to write the book of Revelation. (Revelation 1:9-11)	F	O
7. King Saul persecuted Moses. (1 Samuel 19:10-11)	N	U
8. Jesus told people to pray for their persecutors. (Matthew 5:44)	L	T
9. When people slander you (tell lies), the Bible says to answer kindly. (1 Corinthians 4:13)	*	I
10. King David persecuted Jonathon's son, Mephibosheth. (2 Samuel 9:6-7)	N	A
11. Jesus told people to flee persecution and go to another city. (Matthew 10:23)	L	U
12. The Bible tells us not to be ashamed of persecution, but to praise God. (1 Peter 4:16)	W	A
13. When he was in prison, Peter slept. (Acts 12:6)	A	L
14. Kind Darius wanted the lions to kill Daniel. (Daniel 6:14)	L	Y
15. James, the brother of John, died on a cross. (Acts 12:2)	Y	S

Write the circled letters, in order, to find a message of what to do when persecuted.

___ ___   ___ ___ ___ ___ ___ ___   ___   ___ ___ ___ ___ ___ ___

The uncircled letters tell us something else to do whether persecuted or not.

___ ___ ___ ___   ___ ___ ___ ___ ___ ___ ___ ___ ___ ___ ___

Illogical Reaction

The letters and numbers below are out of order. The code doesn't seem logical. Use the code to discover something Jesus said that only makes sense to believers. Read Matthew 5:11-12a to check your work.

17 9 1 16 16 1 10

6 7 1   22 15 8

21 2 1 5

20 1 15 20 9 1

13 5 16 8 9 3   22 15 8 ,   20 1 7 16 1 4 8 3 1   22 15 8

6 5 10   11 6 9 16 1 9 22   16 6 22   6 9 9

19 13 5 10 16   15 11   1 23 13 9   6 12 6 13 5 16 3

22 15 8   17 1 4 6 8 16 1   15 11   14 1 .

7 1 18 15 13 4 1   6 5 10   17 1   12 9 6 10 ,

17 1 4 6 8 16 1

12 7 1 6 3   13 16

22 15 8 7

7 1 21 6 7 10

13 5   2 1 6 23 1 5 .

1	=	E
2	=	H
3	=	T
4	=	C
5	=	N
6	=	A
7	=	R
8	=	U
9	=	L
10	=	D
11	=	F
12	=	G
13	=	I
14	=	M
15	=	O
16	=	S
17	=	B
18	=	J
19	=	K
20	=	P
21	=	W
22	=	Y
23	=	V

44

SS482

"Jeremiah's Life of Persecution" Puzzle

The prophet Jeremiah suffered much persecution. Complete the puzzle with words that describe Jeremiah's suffering. Look up the Bible verses if you need help.

Across:

3. A large water storage tank that Jeremiah was thrown into (Jeremiah 38:6)

4. Seized to be put in prison (Jeremiah 37:13)

8. Tired (Jeremiah 20:9)

9. Scold or condemn (Jeremiah 15:14)

11. By oneself (Jeremiah 15:17)

12. Evil oaths (Jeremiah 15:10)

14. Mock or tease (Jeremiah 20:8)

Down:

1. Hear (Jeremiah 37:12-14)

2. To be hit repeatedly (Jeremiah 20:2)

5. Confined, not allowed to go places (Jeremiah 36:5)

6. Underground prison (Jeremiah 37:16)

7. To suffer hurt (Jeremiah 15:18)

10. Made fun of (Jeremiah 20:7)

13. Wooden frame used to confine wrists or ankles (Jeremiah 20:2)

SS4829

HEAVEN — POOR IN SPIRIT

COMFORT — MOURN

EARTH — MEEK

FILLED — THIRST AND HUNGER FOR RIGHT

MERCY — MERCIFUL

SEE GOD — PURE IN HEART

CHILD OF GOD — PEACE MAKER

HEAVEN — PERSECUTION

GREAT REWARD — INSULTED

Prophet Wheel

Materials:

2 paper plates
Markers
Glue
Brad fastener

Directions:

1. On the outside rim of a plate, write the names of prophets, clockwise, in the order shown.
2. Cut out the wheel below and glue it to the paper plate, matching "Thrown into a lions' den," with Daniel.
3. Cut a 7" circle from another paper plate. Cut a wedge section out of it to reveal the words on the plate.
4. Print "Persecuted Prophets" on the circle. Attach it to the first plate with a brad fastener.
5. Turn the wheel to learn about prophets who were persecuted.
6. To learn more about what happened to these prophets, look up the Bible verses.

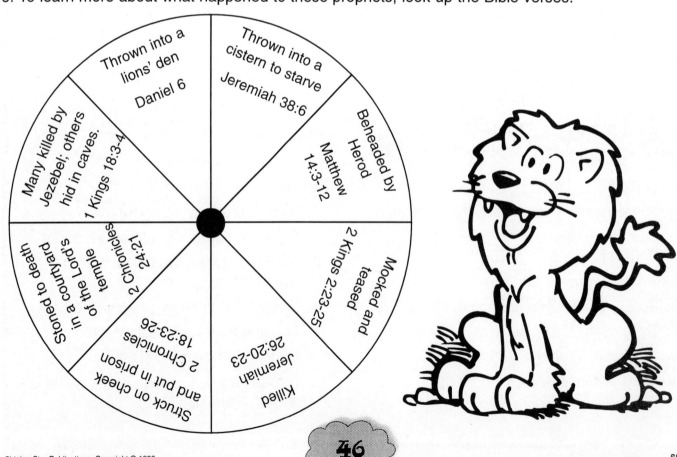

SS4829

Answer Key

Beatitudes Logic Problem ......page 8
Blue, Sally, meek, inherit earth
Red, Luke, pure in heart, see God
Brown, Mary, mourn, comforted
Orange, Juan, Peacemaker, Child of God
Green, Martha, merciful, receive mercy

"Jesus–Our Example"
Match-ups ....page 10
1. b; 2. d; 3. g; 4. i; 5. c; 6. h; 7. a;
8. f; 9. e

Poor in Vowels ....page 11
Blessed are the poor in spirit for theirs
is the kingdom of heaven. Matthew 5:3

Centurion Word Search........page 12

B	L	E	S	S	A	U	T	H	O	R	I	T	Y	E
J	D	C	F	O	L	L	O	W	E	D	A	R	E	D
E	T	A	S	T	O	N	I	S	H	E	D	H	R	E
S	E	R	V	A	N	T	S	T	E	R	U	O	H	L
U	P	E	O	O	R	I	X	E	N	S	L	R	H	A
S	P	D	O	I	R	A	I	T	V	T	H	D	U	E
E	I	B	R	S	F	O	U	N	D	R	I	E	M	H
C	E	N	T	U	R	I	O	N	S	K	E	R	B	I
Y	N	B	E	L	I	E	V	E	D	G	D	S	L	G
O	I	M	P	O	R	T	A	N	T	E	M	O	E	O
F	H	N	E	E	D	E	D	E	A	V	R	E	N	D

Blessed are the poor in spirit for theirs
is the kingdom of heaven.

An <u>important</u> man lived in Capernaum.
He led 100 soldiers who obeyed him.
He was called a <u>centurion</u>. He <u>cared</u>
about the people who worked for him.
One of his <u>servants</u> became very sick;
he could not walk and felt great pain.
The man asked <u>Jesus</u> to help. The
man was very <u>humble</u> and said, "Lord, I
do not <u>deserve</u> to have you come <u>under</u>
my roof." He <u>believed</u> Jesus only
<u>needed</u> to say the word and his servant
would be <u>healed</u>. He explained that he
understood <u>authority</u>. He <u>followed</u> and
gave orders. When he gave <u>orders</u>, he
expected his workers to <u>obey</u>. Jesus
was <u>astonished</u>. "I have not <u>found</u>
anyone in Israel with such great <u>faith</u>,"
Jesus said. He told the centurion to <u>go</u>.
At that very <u>hour</u> the man's servant was
<u>healed</u>.

Spirit of the Game.................page 13
Humble people: poor widow,
centurion, Jesus, Paul, John the Baptist,
Elizabeth, Mary, Job, Moses, Abraham,
King David
Proud people: Pharaoh, King Herod,
Nabal, Moab, Balshazzar, Saul, Haman,
Ananias, and Sapphira

Pyramid Puzzle ....page 15

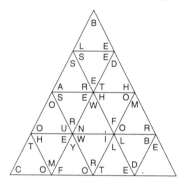

Comforting Word Search ......page 16

F	T	P	E	W	R	I	S	E	E	O	R
T	H	P	B	E	L	I	E	V	E	E	Y
L	I	F	E	W	C	I	I	O	L	L	D
T	H	A	N	K	Y	R	O	L	G	N	E
M	B	C	E	E	R	S	U	S	E	J	R
O	A	H	F	A	I	T	H	I	M	E	U
V	C	R	I	B	B	A	R	O	O	K	O
E	M	I	T	R	O	F	M	O	C	A	P
D	F	S	O	H	R	D	E	P	I	W	T
E	D	T	D	E	A	D	H	A	N	D	S

For they will be comforted

1. sick; 2. poured; 3. wiped; 4. love;
5. Martha; 6. Jesus; 7. Rabbi; 8. friend,
wake; 9. arrive, dead; 10. comfort;
11. rise; 12. life; 13. believe, Christ;
14. moved; 15. wept; 16. kept; 17. see,
glory; 18. thank; 19. benefit; 20. come;
21. hands; 22. faith

Mourning Acrostic ....page 17

J a c o b
J o b
A d a m and E v e
f a t h e r
N a o m i
M a r y
M a r t h a

How to Be Meek ....page 21

h u m b l e
g e n e r o u s
M E E K
c o m p a s s i o n
q u i e t
s u b m i s s i o n
p a t i e n t
u n d e r s t a n d i n g
k i n d
h e a r t

Fractioned Verse...................page 22
Blessed are the meek, for they will
inherit the earth.

Righteousness Crossword Puzzle
page 23

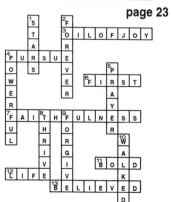

47

SS4829

Answer Key

Seeking Righteousness ....page 25
1. Blessed are those
2. who hunger
3. and thirst
4. for righteousness
5. for they
6. will be filled

Food for Thought ....page 26
bread, water, vine, lamb, wheat

Full Circle Coded Fun ....page 27
1. before; 2. early; 3. sat; 4. dream;
5. town; 6. eel; 7. ribbon; 8. intent;
Blessed are the merciful, for they will be
shown mercy.

**Making Choices
About Helping** ....page 28
1. c; 2. c; 3. a; 4. c; 5. b; 6. c; 7. c;
8. b; 9. b; 10. a

Searching Hearts ....page 33
Blessed are the pure in heart, for they
will see God.

Recipe for a Pure Heart ....page 34
faith, hope, obeying Word

Peacemaker Hall of Fame .....page 39
1. Jonathan; 2. James; 3. Nehemiah;
4. Jacob; 5. Abram; 6. Moses;
7. Abimelech; 8. Abigail; 9. Boaz;
10. Esther; 11. Elders

Singing While Persecuted.....page 40
Blessed are those who are persecuted
because of righteousness, for theirs is
the kingdom of heaven.

"Paul's Problems" Acrostic ..page 42

1. s h i **p** w r e c k e d
2. f l o g g **e** d
3. a r **r** e s t e d
4. l a **s** h e s
5. d r a g g **e** d
6. **c** h a i n e d
7. a c c **u** s e d
8. s **t** r i p p e d
9. s e **i** z e d
10. s **t** o n e d
11. b e a t e **n**

Reactions to Persecution......page 43
True: 1, 3, 4, 6, 8, 9, 11, 12, 13
Be Joyful * always

False: 2, 5, 7, 10, 14, 15
Pray Continually

Illogical Reaction ....page 44
Blessed are you when people insult
you, persecute you, and falsely say all
kinds of evil against you because of me.
Rejoice and be glad, because great is
your reward in heaven.

**"Jeremiah's Life of
Persecution" Puzzle** ....page 45

SS4829